EXTREME STORMS

Paul Mason

A+

Smart Apple Media
P.O. Box 3263
Mankato, MN, 56002

First published in 2011 by
MACMILLAN EDUCATION AUSTRALIA PTY LTD
15–19 Claremont St, South Yarra, Australia 3141

Visit our web site at www.macmillan.com.au or go directly to www.macmillanlibrary.com.au

Associated companies and representatives throughout the world.

Library of Congress Cataloging-in-Publication Data has been applied for.

Publisher: Carmel Heron
Commissioning Editor: Niki Horin
Managing Editor: Vanessa Lanaway
Editors: Philip Bryan and Tim Clarke
Proofreader: Kylie Cockle
Designer: Cristina Neri, Canary Graphic Design
Page layout: Cristina Neri, Canary Graphic Design
Photo researcher: Jes Senbergs (management: Debbie Gallagher)
Illustrator: Peter Bull Art Studio
Production Controller: Vanessa Johnson

Manufactured in China by Macmillan Production (Asia) Ltd.
Kwun Tong, Kowloon, Hong Kong
Supplier Code: CP January 2011

Acknowledgments

The publisher would like to thank the Victoria State Emergency Service for their assistance in reviewing
these manuscripts.

The author and publisher are grateful to the following for permission to reproduce copyright material:

Front cover photograph: Tornado striking buildings, Pampa, Texas, USA, courtesy of Getty Images/Alan
R.Moller.

Photographs courtesy of: AAP Image, **24**; Corbis/Eric Nguyen, **11**; Dreamstime/Denis Radovanovic, **20**;
Getty Images/AFP/Ronaldo Schemidt, **25**, /Richard Bouhet, **23**, /Paula Bronstein, **15**, /NY Daily News, **7**, /
Mario Tama, **21**, **29**; iStockPhoto/Dainis Derics, **13**, /Julia Nichols, **27**, /Michel de Nijs, **12**, /Victor Zastol`skiy,
4; MSF/Eyal Warshawski, **14**, **28**; NOAA, **17**; Photolibrary, **18**; Reuters/Daniel Aguilar, **5**, /Ho New, **16**;
Shutterstock/Dark One, **19**; State Library of Queensland, **22**.

Please Note

At the time of printing, the Internet addresses appearing in this book were correct. Owing to the dynamic
nature of the Internet, however, we cannot guarantee that all these addresses will remain correct.

CONTENTS

DISASTER WORDS

When a word is printed in **bold**, look for its meaning in the "Disaster Words" box.

DISASTER WATCH

Natural disasters can destroy whole areas and kill thousands of people. The only protection from them is to go on disaster watch. This means knowing the warning signs that a disaster might be about to happen, and having a plan for what to do if one strikes.

> We cannot stop natural disasters from happening, but being prepared can help reduce the harm caused by a disaster.

What Are Natural Disasters?

Natural disasters are nature's most damaging events. They include wildfires, earthquakes, extreme storms, floods, tsunamis (say *soon-ah-meez*), and volcanic eruptions.

Preparing for Natural Disasters

Preparing for natural disasters helps us to reduce their effects in three key ways, by:
- increasing our chances of survival
- making our homes as disaster-proof as possible
- reducing the long-term effects of the disaster.

EXTREME STORMS

Extreme storms can blow down houses, flood towns, or bury everything under tons of snow. Whatever dangers these killer storms bring, people who have prepared in advance have the best possible chance of survival.

What Are Extreme Storms?

Extreme storms are our most violent forms of weather. They are different from normal storms because of the amount of damage they cause. This book features three types of extreme storms:

- hurricanes (also called cyclones or typhoons): destructive winds and powerful waves that batter coastal areas
- tornadoes: violently spinning columns of air that usually happen during thunderstorms
- blizzards: blasting winds and tons of snowfall.

Preparing for an Extreme Storm

There are three key ways to prepare for an extreme storm. You must know:

- the warning signs that an extreme storm is on its way
- the safest places to be when an extreme storm arrives
- the challenges facing those who survive.

The strong winds and huge waves of Hurricane Kenna struck Puerto Vallarta in Mexico in October 2002.

WHERE DO EXTREME STORMS HAPPEN?

Each type of extreme storm is more common in some parts of the world than others. Hurricanes affect coastal areas. Blizzards and tornadoes usually affect inland areas.

Hurricanes

There are two key types of extreme hurricane: tropical hurricanes and extra-tropical hurricanes.

Cyclone!

1970: The Bhala Cyclone, the deadliest cyclone ever recorded, struck Bangladesh, killing at least half a million people.

Tropical Hurricanes

Tropical hurricanes start over warmer oceans in the **Tropics**, usually within 10 degrees either side of the **equator**. The areas where they commonly begin include the south-west Pacific Ocean off the Australian coast, the north-east and north-west Pacific Ocean, the Indian Ocean, and the Gulf of Mexico.

Extra-Tropical Hurricanes

Extra-tropical hurricanes are tropical hurricanes that pass over colder water. They are most commonly associated with the northern Atlantic Ocean, passing up the west coast of North America and heading east towards Europe.

DISASTER WORDS

Tropics area where a band of hot weather and high rainfall stretches around the middle of Earth

equator imaginary line running around the middle of Earth

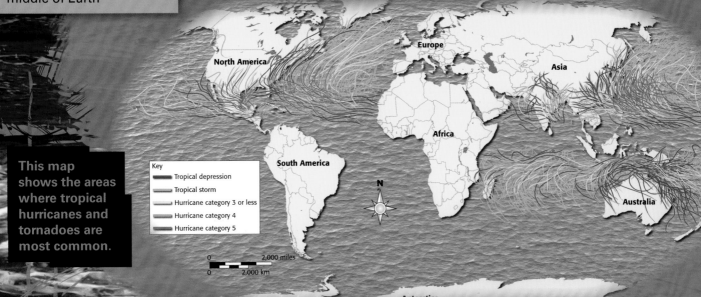

This map shows the areas where tropical hurricanes and tornadoes are most common.

Key
- Tropical depression
- Tropical storm
- Hurricane category 3 or less
- Hurricane category 4
- Hurricane category 5

North America

Europe

Asia

Africa

South America

N

Australia

Antarctica

0   2,000 miles
0   2,000 km

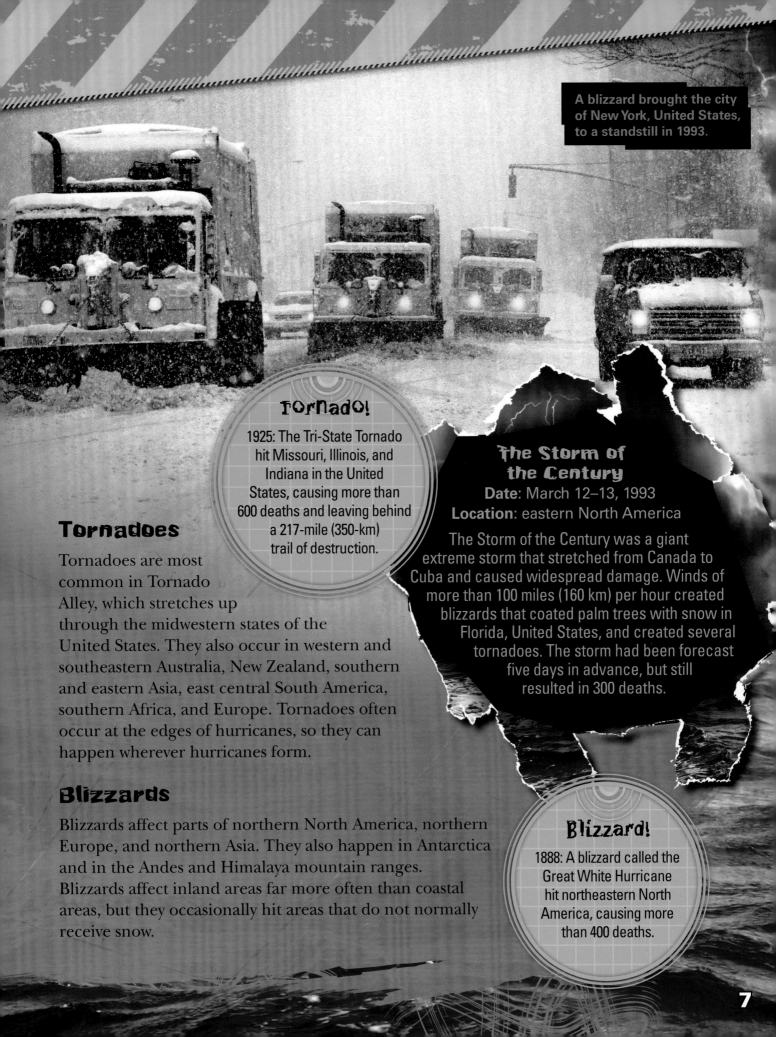

A blizzard brought the city of New York, United States, to a standstill in 1993.

Tornado!

1925: The Tri-State Tornado hit Missouri, Illinois, and Indiana in the United States, causing more than 600 deaths and leaving behind a 217-mile (350-km) trail of destruction.

The Storm of the Century

Date: March 12–13, 1993
Location: eastern North America

The Storm of the Century was a giant extreme storm that stretched from Canada to Cuba and caused widespread damage. Winds of more than 100 miles (160 km) per hour created blizzards that coated palm trees with snow in Florida, United States, and created several tornadoes. The storm had been forecast five days in advance, but still resulted in 300 deaths.

Tornadoes

Tornadoes are most common in Tornado Alley, which stretches up through the midwestern states of the United States. They also occur in western and southeastern Australia, New Zealand, southern and eastern Asia, east central South America, southern Africa, and Europe. Tornadoes often occur at the edges of hurricanes, so they can happen wherever hurricanes form.

Blizzards

Blizzards affect parts of northern North America, northern Europe, and northern Asia. They also happen in Antarctica and in the Andes and Himalaya mountain ranges. Blizzards affect inland areas far more often than coastal areas, but they occasionally hit areas that do not normally receive snow.

Blizzard!

1888: A blizzard called the Great White Hurricane hit northeastern North America, causing more than 400 deaths.

TROPICAL HURRICANES: BEFORE THEY HIT

*Tropical hurricanes are the most damaging extreme storms. They are giant storm systems that form over the ocean. At their heart is a rapidly spinning column of air, with winds of more than 62 miles (100 km) per hour circling around it. These damaging winds bring heavy rain and push a **storm surge** toward land.*

DISASTER WORDS

storm surge rise in sea level caused by an approaching storm

equator imaginary line running around the middle Earth

How Tropical Hurricanes Form

Tropical hurricanes form when seawater 150 feet (50 m) below the surface reaches a temperature of at least 80 °F (27 °C). The warm, moist air above the ocean rises as it is heated by the sun, and colder air rushes in to replace it, creating wind. As the warm air rises, it creates thunderstorms. If several thunderstorms spin together, it creates a tropical hurricane.

Why Hurricanes Spin

Hurricanes spin because winds always blow in a curve, not a straight line. North of the **equator**, winds curve to the right; south of the equator, they curve to the left. Winds blow toward the center of a hurricane from various directions, all of them curving the same way. Eventually these winds increase and start to spin around the center of the storm.

As the hurricane grows, it becomes more powerful and covers an increasingly large area.

Swirling shield of cooling air spreads out

Column of rising air forms the eye of the storm

Around the eye, bands of cloud lift moisture from the ocean

Wah Eh Htoo witnessed the start of the destruction as Cyclone Nargis hit Yangon, Burma (Myanmar), in 2008:

"Trees [had been] ripped from the ground, lying in a tangle across Myanmar's main highway. A large telephone post was uprooted and tossed to the ground three yards (2.7 m) away from our bus."

Hurricane Approaching!

As a tropical hurricane draws near land, the signs that it is approaching become increasingly obvious. All hurricanes behave slightly differently, but most follow the same general pattern.

DISASTER WORDS

squalls sudden, strong gusts of wind and rain

72 Hours before Reaching Land

Ocean swell increases and begins to arrive at regular intervals.

48 Hours before Reaching Land

The sky is likely to be clear of clouds and the swell will increase in size and come more frequently.

36 Hours before Reaching Land

The wind begins to pick up and white clouds will be visible on the horizon.

30 Hours before Reaching Land

Stronger winds cause whitecaps to appear on the ocean surface, and the sky becomes overcast.

24–12 Hours before Reaching Land

Winds and wave heights increase still farther, until it becomes almost impossible to stand outside. **Squalls** increase steadily. These squalls push water from the ocean towards land, causing coastal flooding that is often more deadly and destructive than the hurricane's winds.

Tornadoes happen during extreme storms. They are spinning columns of air, so tightly packed that they look like a tube stretching down from the base of a cloud. The area of the tornado touching the ground is usually less than 260 feet (80 m) across, although it can sometimes be a lot more.

How Tornadoes Form

Most tornadoes form during extreme thunderstorms known as supercell thunderstorms. Supercells contain spinning winds high up in the clouds. Hot air rises inside the supercell, which causes the spinning winds to change from horizontal to vertical. When this happens, a tornado is likely to form.

The column of spinning air inside this thunderstorm has created a tornado.

As the spinning winds get closer to the ground, they increase in speed.

The tornado grows increasingly large and powerful.

The cool air at the heart of the tornado pulls in warm, damp air from nearby.

By the time the narrow funnel of spinning air hits the ground, it can be traveling at anything from 37 mi/h (60 km/h) to 105 mi/h (170 km/h).

Tornado Warning Signs

There are several warning signs that a tornado could be forming, which include:

- the base of a storm cloud rotating
- a cloud with a funnel-shaped bottom
- dust or debris whirling on the ground.

Each of these might show that a tornado funnel is forming inside the cloud.

When a Tornado Hits

When a tornado hits, winds swirl around with a force that can lift cars, trucks, and houses into the air, before smashing them to pieces. Tornadoes move very quickly, zigging and zagging across the land. One minute it seems that the tornado will pass you by, the next it is heading straight at you.

The Super Outbreak

Date: April 3–4, 1974
Location: United States and Canada

The Super Outbreak happened in 1974, when 148 tornadoes hit 13 American states, plus Ontario, Canada, in 24 hours. Altogether, the tornadoes left trails of destruction more than 2,485 miles (4,000 km) long, damaged thousands of homes, and caused more than 300 deaths.

The Fujita Scale

The strength of a tornado, and the damage it is likely to cause, is measured on the Fujita scale.

Fujita Scale	Spinning Speed	Damage
F0	Under 72 mi/h (116 km/h)	Minor damage to trees and buildings
F1	73–112 mi/h (117–180 km/h)	Minor damage to trees and buildings
F2	113–157 mi/h (181–253 km/h)	Vehicles blown around, roofs torn off
F3	158–206 mi/h (254–331 km/h)	Vehicles lifted up, severe damage to weaker buildings
F4	207–260 mi/h (332–418 km/h)	Vehicles thrown into air, brick buildings destroyed
F5	261–318 mi/h (419–512 km/h)	Most buildings destroyed
F6	319–379 mi/h (512–610 km/h)	Complete destruction

An approaching tornado has a distinctive funnel-shaped bottom.

BLIZZARDS: BEFORE THEY HIT

Blizzards are severe storms that feature high winds, heavy snowfall, and low temperatures. Their key characteristic – and what makes them different from ordinary snowstorms – is the strength of the wind. In the United States, a snowstorm is defined as a blizzard if the winds are more than 35 miles (56 km) per hour.

How Blizzards Form

Blizzards form when warm air from the **Tropics** meets cold air over land. This damp tropical air becomes colder and its moisture turns to snow. The result is heavy snow, combined with extremely high winds as the warm air and cold air rush together.

EYEWITNESS WORDS

Steve saw a major problem caused by a blizzard in Virginia, United States, in December 2009:

"People who were driving small cars were slipping and sliding and crashing into parked cars."

DISASTER WORDS

Tropics area where a band of hot weather and high rainfall stretches around the middle of Earth

Before a blizzard hits, warm air and cold air rush together over the land, creating dramatic cloud formations that will release heavy snow.

Pedestrians struggle to find a safe way through the heavy snowfall of a blizzard in Finland.

Blizzard Warning Signs

If you have this combination of weather conditions, a blizzard could be about to hit:

- huge banks of clouds forming
- strong winds
- air temperature below 40 °F (4.5 °C).

When a Blizzard Hits

When a blizzard hits, high winds drive heavy snowfall through the air. The wind picks up snow that has already fallen and blows icy crystals against people's faces. The swirling snow makes it hard for pedestrians and drivers to see, and piles up against buildings and other obstacles, forming deep snowdrifts.

The Great Blizzard of 1999

Date: January 2–4, 1999
Location: United States and Canada

The Great Blizzard of 1999 was the second-worst blizzard to hit North America in the twentieth century. Despite knowing the storm was coming, communities across the Midwest were cut off for days, and travel became impossible for many people. There were 73 blizzard-related deaths.

WHAT DAMAGE DO EXTREME STORMS CAUSE?

Extreme storms have strong winds: more than 62 miles (100 km) per hour for hurricanes and tornadoes, and more than 35 miles (56 km) per hour for blizzards. These winds kill people and animals, and damage the natural environment. However, each kind of storm has further damaging effects.

DISASTER WORDS

storm surge rise in sea level caused by an approaching storm

Hurricane Damage

A hurricane's strong winds tear down buildings and turn anything not tied down into a deadly flying object. However, flooding caused by heavy rain and the **storm surge** causes even greater damage.

EYEWITNESS WORDS

Hurricane Ivan caused terrible damage when it hit Grand Cayman Island in the Caribbean in 2004:

"It is total devastation, whole apartments have been washed away. I have friends that have nothing but the clothing they are wearing."

Human Impact

Worldwide, 90 percent of people killed by hurricanes die because of flooding. The water drowns people and leaves thousands homeless and hungry. Floodwater contains the bodies of dead animals and people, and spreads disease.

Environmental Impact

Hurricanes destroy animals' homes, and some animals drown or die from disease. Others starve because they cannot find enough to eat. Land flooded by seawater becomes salty and will not be good for growing crops.

After a hurricane struck Bangladesh in 2007, thousands of people had to take refuge in emergency shelters. As people were crowded together, diseases could spread quickly.

If a blizzard hits an area where it does not normally snow, livestock need to be protected from the cold or moved to a warmer area.

Tornado Damage

Tornadoes cause damage because of their high wind speeds.

Human Impact

Most people who die in tornadoes are killed when buildings and bridges collapse, or when they are hit by flying objects. Survivors are likely to find damaged buildings and vehicles, and might be left homeless.

Environmental Impact

Crops, livestock, and wildlife in the path of a tornado are unlikely to survive.

Blizzard Damage

Blizzards can be extremely destructive. The biggest danger is dealing with the sudden change in temperature and conditions.

Human Impact

Blizzards make travel difficult. The ice, snow, and lack of visibility increase the risk of having a car accident or freezing to death in a car. Food deliveries and other services shut down temporarily.

Environmental Impact

Blizzards usually happen in areas where the wildlife, trees, and plants can cope with the snowy conditions. Elsewhere, low temperatures and snow kill plants and animals that are used to a warmer climate.

FORECASTING EXTREME STORMS

Today's advances in technology and weather forecasting make it easier than ever to predict the formation of hurricanes, blizzards, and tornadoes. Once a storm has been forecast, TV, radio, and the Internet are used to let people know that it is on its way.

Storm-Forecasting Technology

Meteorologists use modern technology, such as satellites and radar, to predict whether extreme storms will happen.

Satellite Images

Satellite images are weather "snapshots" taken from space using special cameras. They are then beamed back to Earth, allowing meteorologists to see what the weather is doing over a huge area. Special infrared images can be used at night or for measuring the strength of a tropical hurricane.

GULF OF MEXICO

MEXICO

PACIFIC OCEAN

GUATEMALA

Hurricane Rick -->

This satellite photo shows Hurricane Rick approaching the west coast of Central America in October, 2009.

Cyclone Tracy

Date: December 24–25, 1974
Location: Darwin, Australia

Cyclone Tracy was packed into a smaller area than any other recorded cyclone. It was less than 31 miles (50 km) wide – but extremely violent. Although people knew the cyclone was coming, 71 people died. Roughly 70 percent of Darwin's buildings were destroyed, and 80 percent of Darwin's residents were left homeless.

Radar

A weather radar can detect **precipitation** 124 miles (200 km) away, and shows more detail than a satellite image. A sequence of radar images shows how the precipitation is behaving – whether it is increasing, and how fast it is moving.

Measuring Devices

Meteorologists rely on a variety of measuring devices, most of which work automatically and transmit their results to a weather-center computer. Most storm forecasts combine information from:

- barometers, which measure air pressure: low air pressure is associated with strong winds, so a sharp drop in air pressure shows a storm could be on the way
- anemometers measuring wind speed, and a wind vane, which measures wind direction
- thermometers for measuring temperature
- rain gauges, which show how much precipitation has fallen
- weather balloons, which measure air pressure and wind speed at various heights (winds very high in the atmosphere affect the direction in which the storm will travel).

DISASTER WORDS
precipitation moisture falling from clouds, usually as rain or snow

MONITORING EXTREME STORMS

Once an extreme storm has been detected, weather forecasters predict how it is likely to behave. They try to work out the direction it will travel, and whether it will become stronger or weaker. This allows them to give warnings to people who could be in the storm's path.

Predicting Hurricane and Blizzard Behavior

Meteorologists use their knowledge of nearby weather systems and winds to accurately predict the course and strength of hurricanes and blizzards.

Nearby Weather Systems

Hurricanes and blizzards are **low-pressure** weather systems. Meteorologists analyze the wind movement, direction, and speed of these systems to predict what will happen if two low-pressure systems combine, or if a low-pressure system will have to move around a high-pressure system.

This satellite image shows a hurricane approaching the southern United States.

High-Level Winds

High above Earth's surface, streams of wind blow in curving paths. When a large weather system, such as a hurricane, moves below one of these streams of wind, it affects the storm's direction. Meteorologists know where these streams of wind are and how fast they are moving, and can predict how they will affect the direction of the storm.

Changes of Strength

Hurricanes and blizzards increase in strength as long as the conditions that feed them are available in increasing amounts. A hurricane, for example, loses strength if it moves over land because the warm ocean and moist air that feed it are no longer present.

Predicting Tornado Behavior

It is hard to predict how a tornado will behave once it has formed, as it can change direction suddenly without warning. However, forecasters know that once a tornado begins to run out of the warm air that powers it, it begins to lose strength, and that most tornadoes last only a few minutes.

Cyclone Larry
Date: March 18–21, 2006
Location: Queensland, Australia

Cyclone Larry was one of the most powerful extreme storms ever to hit Australia. Gusts of wind were measured at 182 miles (294 km) per hour. Buildings were destroyed, along with 80 percent of Australia's banana crop.

Tornadoes that form over seas or lakes are called waterspouts.

BEFORE AN EXTREME STORM STRIKES

Once **meteorologists** have forecast that an extreme storm is on its way, the authorities prepare for when it will strike. They make sure people have been warned that the storm is coming, issue advice, and get ready to help the storm's victims in the aftermath.

Storm Warnings

One of the first jobs for meteorologists and the authorities is to release warnings that an extreme storm is on its way.

Hurricane and Blizzard Warnings

Hurricanes and blizzards can be predicted hours or even days in advance. Warnings that the storm is coming will be given in newspapers, and broadcast on TV and radio, and via the Internet.

Tornado Warnings

Tornado warnings can only be given at very short notice, although forecasters know in advance that the weather that might lead to tornadoes is on its way.

In some states of the United States, tornado sirens give people a short warning that a tornado is nearby.

The siren goes off when...

A tornado has been spotted!

Tightly rotating cloud formations have been seen!

Weather radar says a tornado is forming inside a storm cloud!

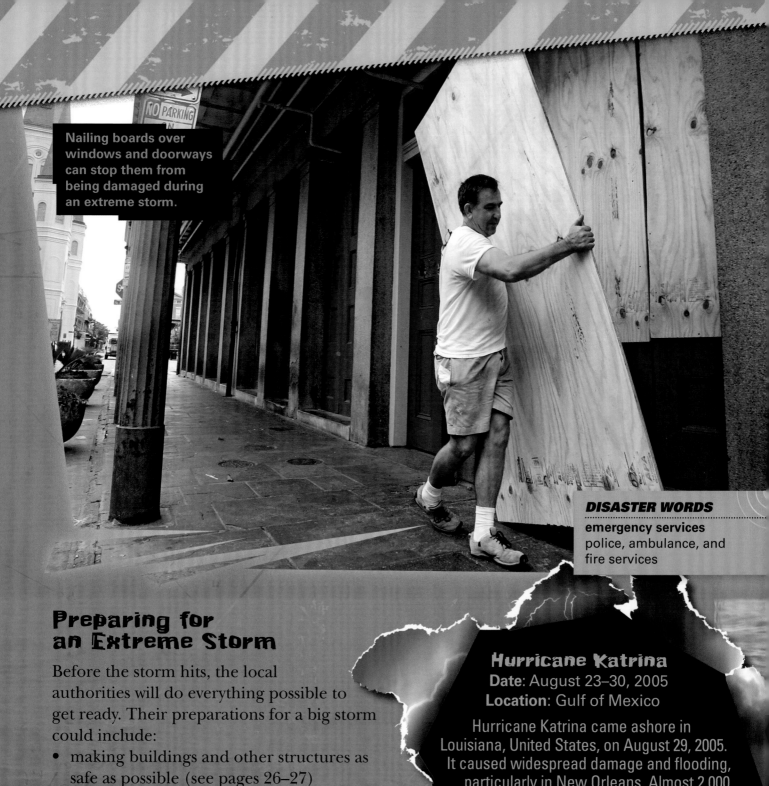

Nailing boards over windows and doorways can stop them from being damaged during an extreme storm.

DISASTER WORDS
emergency services
police, ambulance, and fire services

Preparing for an Extreme Storm

Before the storm hits, the local authorities will do everything possible to get ready. Their preparations for a big storm could include:

- making buildings and other structures as safe as possible (see pages 26–27)
- putting the **emergency services** on standby. Once the storm has begun, everyone will have to wait it out in a secure place. However, as soon as it is safe, the emergency services will be needed to help the storm's victims.
- preparing supplies of food, water, and temporary shelters, which will be desperately needed by the survivors.

Hurricane Katrina
Date: August 23–30, 2005
Location: Gulf of Mexico

Hurricane Katrina came ashore in Louisiana, United States, on August 29, 2005. It caused widespread damage and flooding, particularly in New Orleans. Almost 2,000 people were killed. Afterward, there were many claims that the authorities had not been properly prepared and that the damage was worse than it should have been.

ARE YOU AT RISK?

Are you and your family at risk from an extreme storm? Your local library and council offices, and the Internet, are good places to start to investigate the area where you are living or staying.

Key Questions

Measure the risk from an extreme storm by asking key questions about an area's storm history, and whether there are preparations in place in case an extreme storm strikes. Ask the following questions about where you live, or where you are holidaying.

The Bathurst Bay Hurricane

Date: March 4, 1899
Location: Queensland, Australia

The Bathurst Bay hurricane (also called Cyclone Mahina) hit Bathurst Bay in Queensland, Australia, without warning, wrecking the boats of the local pearling fleet. At least 307 sailors were killed, and only four survived. More than 100 Indigenous Australians were also killed.

Are You in an Area Where Extreme Storms Have Happened in the Past?

Although extreme storms can happen anywhere, they are more frequent in some places than others. For example, north-eastern Australia is regularly hit by cyclones, and Tornado Alley in the United States is regularly hit by tornadoes.

What Time of Year Do the Storms Happen?

The risk of extreme storms is higher at certain times of year. In north-eastern Australia, for example, "cyclone season" runs from November to April. In Tornado Alley in the United States, tornadoes are most likely from April to June.

North-eastern Australia has been hit by extreme storms in the past, such as Cyclone Mahina in 1899, the path of which is shown by this old map. This means that the area is at risk of extreme storms today.

Is Your Location Sheltered?

High winds are one of the most destructive features of extreme storms. If your building is sheltered by a hill, or sheltered by a stronger, taller building, this can reduce the risks from an extreme storm.

Are You Near the Coast?

Hurricanes bring flooding, as **storm surges** combine with heavy rain. Anyone close to the coast or near sea level is at greater risk than people on higher ground.

Do You Live in a Town or City, or Is Your Home Isolated?

An extreme storm poses a smaller threat in a town or city, as there is greater likelihood of shelter and of help being available. In an isolated location, you will have to cope with the storm alone.

Are You Somewhere that Is Designed to Withstand Extreme Weather?

Modern building techniques can be used to make structures able to cope with tremendous forces. If these techniques have been used, extreme storms are likely to cause less damage.

DISASTER WORDS

storm surges rises in sea level caused by an approaching storm

This building on the island of Saint-Paul de la Reunion was right on the coast, so was torn down by waves from Cyclone Gamede in February, 2007.

TOP TIPS FOR REDUCING RISK

Governments and local councils do all they can to protect people from extreme storms. However, it is also important that you take whatever action you can to keep yourself safe. What can you and your family do if you are somewhere at risk from extreme storms?

Watch for Warnings

Make sure you recognize the storm-rating systems. For example, what is meant by a "category 3 hurricane?" Familiarize yourself with any warning signals or sirens that might be set off, and be alert for signs of extreme storms.

Preparing an Emergency Plan

An emergency plan is a plan detailing what everyone will do if an extreme storm happens. Start by discussing the plan with your family. The plan should include:

- the location of the family's safest place; for example, a basement, or a public building on higher ground
- your evacuation route (if you decide to evacuate), including where you will head for
- any jobs that people should do before going to the safe place or evacuating; for example, fastening storm shutters on windows.

After a hurricane hit Wisconsin, United States, in 2002, firefighters checked people's basements to see if any survivors had taken refuge.

Follow the Storm's Movements

Keep a map of your area nearby, and follow the storm's movement on weather bulletins to see if it is getting closer. If it looks like the storm is approaching, you can start to carry out part of your emergency plan, such as protecting your home.

E-mail Crucial Documents

E-mail scans of important documents, such as insurance information, to yourself at a web-based e-mail service. That way you will not lose the information that the documents contain.

Extreme Storm Myths

Believing some of these myths about extreme storms could cost you your life.

1 *Tornadoes always move northeasterly.*

False! Tornadoes can move in any direction.

2 *Tornadoes do not affect cities.*

False! Tornadoes regularly hit cities: New York, United States, has been hit twice in recent years.

3 *Hurricanes only strike during "hurricane season."*

False! That is when hurricanes are most likely, but they can also strike at other times of year.

4 *It is safe to go outside in the **eye** of a storm.*

False! Storms move very quickly, and being caught outside would be fatal.

5 *Opening the windows on the side away from the wind will stop the house exploding.*

False! It will let the wind in, which is likely to cause greater damage.

Storm shutters or nailed-down plywood can be used to protect windows during an extreme storm.

WHAT YOU CAN DO IF AN EXTREME STORM HAPPENS

If an extreme storm hits, it is important to stay calm and think clearly. As the storm approaches, there will be preparations your family can make to keep your home as secure as possible. Once the storm is upon you, take shelter.

After the Warnings

Once you know that an extreme storm is on its way, you may have a little time to make last-minute preparations.

Before a Hurricane or Blizzard Hits

Before a hurricane or blizzard hits, there may be a few hours that your family can use to prepare. Some of the key things to do are shown in the labels below. Never stay outside during the storm trying to finish these jobs. As soon as conditions become dangerous, move to shelter.

Preparing your home will minimize the damage caused by an extreme storm.

If flooding threatens, move essential items and supplies as far above the ground as possible.

Bring pets indoors.

Secure loose objects or bring them indoors.

Check the roof is in good condition.

Block any draughty gaps.

Close storm shutters, or use sheets of plywood to cover windows.

In a tornado, supplies are safest in the basement or at the center of the house.

Park vehicles in a sheltered position.

Before a Tornado Hits

Tornadoes may approach at high speed and with very little warning. If you can see a tornado, there is no time for preparation. Take cover immediately in the nearest, most secure location.

When the Storm Arrives

As soon as the wind picks up and the rain or snow begins to fall, find shelter. In extreme high winds, the safest place in a house is the basement. If there is no basement, go to a strong-walled room in the middle of the ground floor. Stay away from windows, which might be blown in.

Three days' supply of water (4 quarts [4 L] per person per day) and food that will not spoil

Warm clothes, and a blanket or sleeping bag per person

If your home is at risk from extreme storms, have a storm emergency kit ready to take wherever you plan to shelter.

First-aid kit, including essential medicines

Wind-up radio and torch

Charged cell phone containing emergency and important numbers

AFTER AN EXTREME STORM

The danger from an extreme storm does not disappear as soon as the storm passes. People may need medical help, food, water, and shelter. Damaged buildings, flooding, or ice and snow may be hazards.

Helping Storm Victims

People who have lived through an extreme storm may need a variety of different kinds of help, depending on the type of storm.

Food and Supplies

After a blizzard or hurricane, snow or flooding can make travel difficult for several days. Elderly people may not be able to get out for food and other supplies. They will need help from friends and neighbors. Supplies may not reach the stores, so everyone has to rely on their emergency food supplies.

After Cyclone Nargis struck Burma in 2008, the survivors had to queue to receive emergency food and water supplies.

After Hurricane Katrina flooded New Orleans, United States, in 2005, more than 20,000 people were forced to take shelter in the Louisiana Superdome.

Shelter

Extreme storms damage homes and other buildings, so people may need help finding somewhere to sleep. They might stay with friends and neighbors or – if the damage is extensive – they might have to move to temporary shelters, such as tent villages set up by the authorities.

Further Hazards

The storm can leave behind wreckage and other hazards. Among the dangers to watch out for are:

- buildings and structures that have been damaged, and need either to be repaired to make them safe, or knocked down
- power cables that have broken loose
- flood water, which contains dangers such as unexpectedly deep water, sharp wreckage, poisonous chemicals, and diseases
- snow and ice after a blizzard make moving about hazardous, causing injuries from car accidents and falls.

 EYEWITNESS WORDS

A 29-year-old man witnessed the aftermath of Cyclone Nargis, which hit Myanmar in May 2008:

"Water is the main problem for people now. Everybody is talking about the shortage of water .... At the drinking-water company, people are queuing for water to drink."

QUIZ: DO YOU KNOW WHAT TO DO?

Now that you have read about extreme storms, would you have a better chance of surviving if one happened near you? Test yourself using this quiz.

1 When are you most likely to see a tornado?

a When there is a big thunderstorm.
b In the morning.
c During winter.

2 How should you prepare your home's windows if a hurricane or tornado threatens?

a Close the storm shutters on all windows, or nail plywood over them.
b Put parcel tape crosses across the glass.
c Close the windows nearest the storm, and open the ones on the other side of the house.

3 In extreme high winds, where is the safest place to take shelter?

a In the basement, or an inside ground-floor room.
b On the side of the building farthest from the wind.
c Upstairs, so you can look out of the window and see the storm approaching.

4 You spot a cloud with a swirling cone shape at the bottom. Do you say:

a "Take cover, everyone! There's a tornado coming!"
b "Mom! Bring me my camera!"
c "That's weird", then carry on with what you were doing.

5 What are you most likely to need after the storm has passed?

a Food, water, warm clothing, and shelter.
b A computer for uploading your storm photos to Facebook.
c A shower.

How did you do?

Mostly b or c answers: You had better read this book again, or hope that you never experience an extreme storm. At the moment, you would be at great risk.

Mostly or all a answers: Not only would you have the best possible chance of surviving, you might also be able to help other people stay safe during a storm.

DISASTER WATCHING ON THE WEB

Being on disaster watch means being prepared. It also means knowing where to get information ahead of a disaster, knowing how disasters happen, receiving disaster warnings, and getting updates on what is happening after a disaster has struck.

Find out More about Extreme Storms

Check out these web sites to find out more about extreme storms.

- **www.howstuffworks.com**
  This site has lots of information about different kinds of extreme storms, how they are formed, and their effects.
- **www.weatherwizkids.com**
  This site has a lot of good information about tornadoes, hurricanes, and winter storms. There is an animation in the "hurricane" section of how storm surges wash away some houses near the sea, but not others.
- **www.clearlyexplained.com**
  This site has basic information about cyclones, plus links to several other good web sites.

Extreme Storms near you

How would an extreme storm affect your local area, and what warning might you get? To find out, contact your local government and see whether:

- they have an emergency plan for extreme storms, and
- they know of a web site you can look at for storm warnings.

Your local library might also be able to help you find this information.

Alternatively, these web sites might be able to steer you toward local information:

- **www.weather.gov** The US National Weather Service carries a live map showing all kinds of weather-related hazards (including flooding) in the United States.
- **www.pdc.org** has a live map of current disasters (including earthquakes, volcanoes, floods, and extreme storms), which you can click on to find out more. There is also an excellent resources section, with information about extreme storms and other disasters.

INDEX